I0824280

BEACH LANE BOOKS
An imprint of Simon & Schuster Children's Publishing Division
1230 Avenue of the Americas, New York, New York 10020

Book design by Lauren Rille

The text for this book was set in Catalina Clemente.
The illustrations for this book were rendered in gouache watercolor and finished digitally.
Manufactured in China
1025 SCP
First Edition
10 9 8 7 6 5 4 3 2 1
CIP data for this book is available from the Library of Congress.
ISBN 9781665961042
ISBN 9781665961059 (ebook)

Just One Oak

What a Single Tree Can Be

Written by Maria Gianferrari

Illustrated by Diana Sudyka

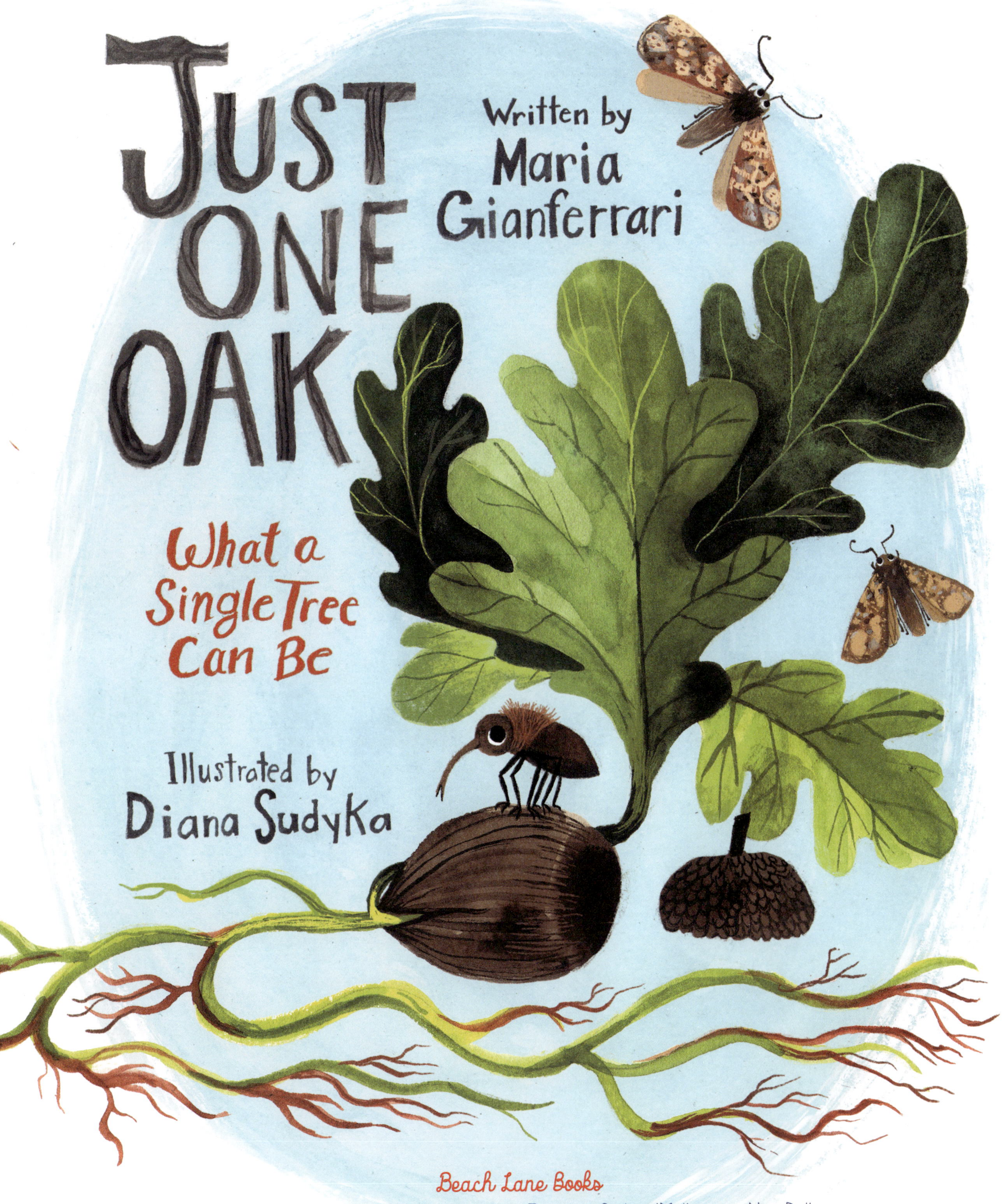

Beach Lane Books

New York Amsterdam/Antwerp London Toronto Sydney/Melbourne New Delhi

Just one oak...
from the tip
of its crown
down to the ground,
with roots all around,
sustains so very
many creatures,
Blue jay
Gray squirrel
Field mice
Bur oak acorn
from the teeny-tiny . . .

Screech owl
Black bear
Bur oak
Chicken-of-the-woods
to the big and mighty.

Just one oak...

clings to its crown
of leaves
the winter through.

Leaves swirl off in spring,
right when they're needed most.

Marcescence (mahr-CESS-ense), when a tree's leaves brown and wither in autumn but still remain on the tree, may be a tree's defense against browsers like deer. Scientists think the bitter brown leaves may prevent animals from eating the tree's leaf buds in spring. With the help of decomposers, freshly fallen leaves add nutrition to the soil.

Just one oak...

with leaves rolled, folded,
tied, tented, and sticky
with silk, can be a home—

and a dining room.

Duskywing skippers are a type of butterfly, and oak leafrollers are a type of moth, both of which specialize in feeding on oak trees. As caterpillars, they build shelters by folding oak leaves and binding them with silk so they can dine out of sight of predators. Oak trees sustain more moths and butterflies than other native tree species.

Just one oak...

shelters sleepy insects
nestling in the nooks
of its shaggy bark
and branches—

until spring.

In the fall, caterpillars of all kinds, especially inchworms, prepare to overwinter in oaks by crawling into bark crannies or onto branches. Glycerin, a kind of nature's antifreeze, helps keep their cells from bursting. Overwintering insects are food sources for predatory spiders and songbirds such as chickadees, tufted titmice, creepers, woodpeckers, and nuthatches. Approximately half of a chickadee's winter diet consists of insects. In spring, caterpillars are easy to catch, the perfect high-fat food for growing chicks.

Just one oak...

drilled by woodpeckers
and filled with acorns,
becomes a granary—

a winter food supply.

Found in the western United States, acorn woodpeckers are social birds that live together in family groups and cooperatively raise their young. Beginning in autumn, they drill holes in granary trees, adding more holes and acorns each season for winter storage. A single tree may have as many as 50,000 acorn-filled holes!

Just one oak...

loses lots of leaves.
Leaf litter,
the blanket beneath its boughs,
saves and sustains—

nourishes
and nurtures
above . . .

The blanket of fallen oak leaves on the ground is known as duff, or leaf litter. Leaf litter creates an ideal environment for a variety of recyclers and decomposers called the brown food web. Oak leaves are dense and contain bitter chemical compounds called tannins. They slowly decompose over time, creating humid conditions that feed a multitude of small animals.

and below.

Stick bug
Wood louse
Springtail
Mites
Centipede
Fungal hyphae

Oak leaf litter bolsters bacteria and fungi populations, which decompose dead plant matter and recycle it into food. This provides nourishment for surrounding species, including their own predators.

Just one Oak...

began as a taproot diving down;
lateral roots branch,
spreading sideways near the soil's surface—

farther than
the canopy is wide.

From the taproot, lateral roots branch and extend horizontally in shallow soil, up to three times beyond the oak's canopy, giving it support. They then form a finer cluster of roots so that the oak can soak up moisture and nutrients from the soil.

Just one Oak...

produces fruits called acorns. Each acorn can be a home for one—

or a house for hundreds.

The female acorn weevil chews a hole in an acorn, lays an egg, then seals the acorn's surface with poop. The larva eats the acorn's innards for two long months as it grows inside. When the acorn falls from the tree, the larva exits, tunneling in soil where it will remain for two years until full-grown. Then it will seek a mate, find an acorn, and begin the process again. The tiny hole bored by an acorn weevil is big enough to house hundreds of ants, sheltering them from predators.

Just one Oak...

and its little acorns ensure that wildlife of all kinds survive cold winters.

Those little acorns are . . .

You may know that gray squirrels cache acorns for those cold winter days, but other animals and birds eat acorns too. Red squirrels, flying squirrels, mice, voles, and chipmunks survive on acorns; so do opossums, rabbits, and raccoons. Even bigger mammals such as red foxes, gray foxes, and coyotes depend on acorns. Black bears gorge on acorns before hibernating. In late fall, about 75 percent of a white-tailed deer's diet consists of acorns, while a wild boar's diet is approximately 70 percent acorns. More than 100 vertebrate species are known to eat acorns. Acorns are the main winter diet for a multitude of birds—from wild turkeys, woodpeckers, and wood ducks to crows and quails and songbirds like tufted titmice, towhees, and more.

a nutritious superfood!

Acorns are highly nutritious. They contain protein, carbohydrates, fat, and vitamins and minerals like calcium and potassium. Acorns give animals the energy they need to stay warm and survive during winter.

Just one blue jay...
buries thousands of acorns,
which may one day become—

a new grove of oaks.

A single blue jay can gather and bury more than 4,000 acorns each fall. Since a blue jay may remember only some acorn locations, many acorns will sprout. Over the course of its life, a blue jay may plant thousands of trees each year.

Just one oak...

sometimes supplies thousands of acorns during an acorn masting—

a fallen feast.

When an oak produces a bumper crop, a higher-than-usual number of acorns, it's known as a masting. During mast years, thousands of acorns may fall. This abundant food supply leads to increased wildlife populations. The following year, trees may not fruit, and wildlife populations may decrease. Mastings occur every two to five years.

Just one Oak...

gifts millions of acorns
in its lifetime.

A mature oak tree can produce as many as three million acorns over the course of its life.

Just one oak...

creates
a microclimate,

cleaning the air,
slowing winds,
warming in winter—

and shading in summer.

Oaks improve air quality by absorbing carbon dioxide and creating oxygen. Their canopies help block wind during storms; they absorb sun in winter and create shade in summer. When planted in cities, oaks and other trees can help lessen heat island effect—a condition where pavement, buildings, and other artificial surfaces absorb and retain heat.

Just one oak...

prevents flooding and topsoil erosion—

like a sponge in a storm.

Thousands of gallons of water can be absorbed by oak leaf litter and its underlying humus, the organic material in soil. The leaf litter helps water seep underground to fill up water tables and slows water flow, preventing both flooding and erosion. Leaf litter can also act as a filter, removing excess fertilizers and even some heavy metals.

From the tip
of its crown

down to the ground,
with roots all around . . .

JUST ONE

OAK
is beautiful and bountiful to all.

HOORAY FOR THE HUMBLE OAK!

Oak trees are a keystone species, which means that many other species depend on them for survival. In North America, oaks support more forms of life than any other tree family, from microscopic creatures and fungi in the soil and leaf litter to insects, spiders, birds, and a host of mammals. Oaks alone sustain over 950 species of caterpillars nationwide. Most of them (94 percent) either pupate under the soil or spin cocoons in the leaf litter.

IN PRAISE OF THE LEAF

The main job of a leaf is to help make food for a tree. Leaves contain chlorophyll, a pigment that gives them their green color. Chlorophyll helps leaves use sunlight, water, and carbon dioxide to make food (sugar and oxygen) for the tree. This process is called photosynthesis.

Leaves contain stomata, tiny holes to help them breathe. Stomata take in carbon dioxide, and release oxygen and water vapor. To help balance water loss, leaves open and close their stomata.

VARIATIONS ON AN OAK LEAF

Leaves at the top of a tree receive direct exposure to the sun, so they need less surface area to collect sunlight. As a result, leaves at the top of a tree are smaller and have more deeply cut lobes, which helps prevent overheating. The opposite is true for the bottom of the tree—the leaves have fewer lobes since they require more surface area to collect sunlight due to shade from the upper canopy and branches.

COMMON OAK LEAF SHAPES

ANATOMY OF AN ACORN

Acorns are the fruit of an oak tree. They drop from trees in the fall and are spread by birds and mammals. This is called dispersal. There are two basic acorn shapes: round-shaped, more easily carried by mammals such as chipmunks, squirrels, and deer, and football-shaped, better adapted for a bird's beak.

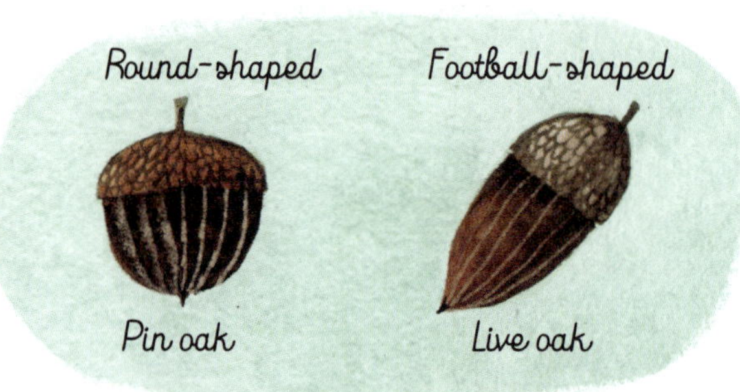

HOW YOU CAN HELP: OAK TREE REGENERATION

One mature oak tree can help fight climate change by absorbing nearly 50 pounds (22 kilograms) of carbon per year! You can grow an oak from an acorn. Here's how:

Consult Homegrown National Park to find your ecoregion: homegrownnationalpark.org/ecoregion-finder/. Then visit the "North American Keystone Plants" page to find the native oaks in your area: homegrownnationalpark.org/keystone-plants/

In the fall, collect acorns from native oak species in your community.

Native oaks (and other plants) are best because they:

- ensure the health of our ecosystems.
- support a wide variety of animals, plants, fungi, and microorganisms, which create healthy soil, clean air, and food sources for wildlife. More natives means more biodiversity.
- are often harmed or destroyed by invasive, or non-native, species. Non-native species spread rapidly and compete with native species for valuable resources.

Is your acorn from a red oak (leaves with pointed lobes) or a white oak (leaves with rounded lobes)?

If it's a red oak:

- It will sprout in the spring.
- Place your acorn in a plastic bag. Add peat mix or sawdust. Seal and store it in your refrigerator at 40 degrees.
- In the spring, add soil and plant the acorn sideways in a flowerpot. Place it outside in a sunny area.

If it's a white oak:

- It will sprout in the fall.
- Add soil to a flowerpot, and plant your acorn sideways. Store it in a cool place such as a garage or a shed. Water it once a month.
- If you don't have a garage or a shed, place it outside and cover it to protect it from hungry critters.
- In the spring, place it in a sunny spot outside.

Once your acorn seedlings are about twelve inches tall, plant them in your yard, at your school, or in your neighborhood. Oaks grow best together in groves about ten feet apart. Their roots will eventually interlock, which will protect them from damaging winds.

MORE WAYS TO ROOT FOR OAKS

- Collect acorns with your friends, plant them in pots, and give them as holiday or birthday gifts!
- Keep the ground soft beneath oak trees with plantings rather than lawn grass and mulch to support the caterpillar life cycle and food web. In the fall, leave the leaves.
- Distribute acorns or oak seedlings for planting in your neighborhood—in city and town parks, public gardens, schools, places of worship, local businesses, and more!
- Organize volunteers to collect acorns for your local arboretum or nature conservancy organization and their oak regeneration projects.

OAK TREE LIFE CYCLE

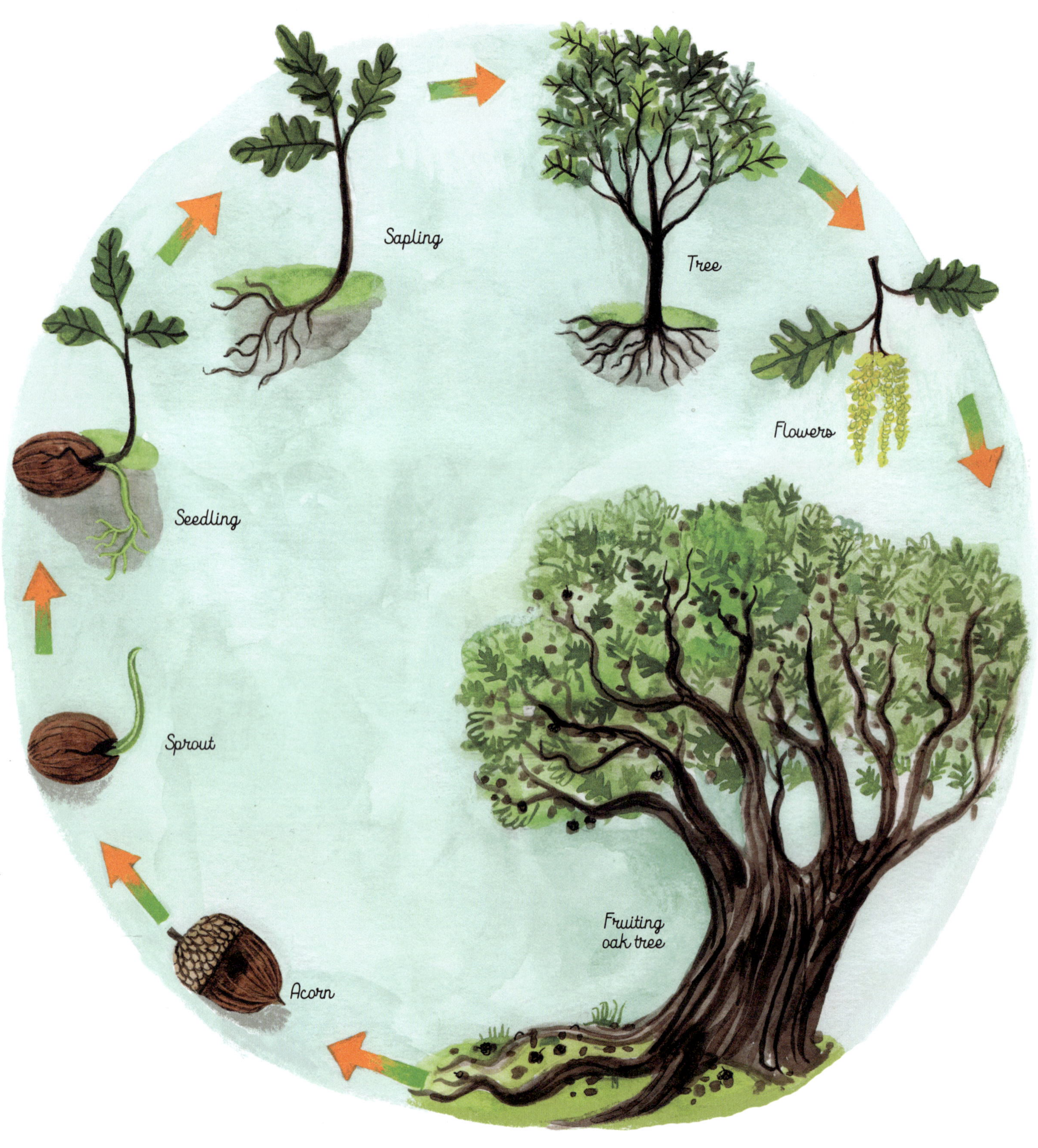

SOURCES

Hipp, Andrew L. *Oak Origins: From Acorns to Species and the Tree of Life.* Chicago: University of Chicago Press, 2024.

Nix, Steve. "Guide to Common Oak Trees of North America." Treehugger, April 29, 2021. treehugger.com/guide-to-common-oak-trees-of-north-america-1343226.

Rindy, Jenna, et al. "Urban Trees Are Sinks for Soot: Elemental Carbon Accumulation by Two Widespread Oak Species." Environmental Science & Technology, August 12, 2019. pubs.acs.org/doi/10.1021/acs.est.9b02844#.

Tallamy, Douglas W. "The Nature of Oaks." Homegrown National Park, video. homegrownnationalpark.org/the-nature-of-oaks/.

Tallamy, Douglas W. *The Nature of Oaks: The Rich Ecology of Our Most Essential Native Trees.* Portland: Timber Press, 2021.

Wohlleben, Peter. *The Hidden Life of Trees: What They Feel, How They Communicate.* Vancouver: Greystone Books, 2016.

FURTHER READING FOR KIDS

Carlson-Berne, Emma. *The Story of an Oak Tree: It Starts with an Acorn.* Minneapolis: Lerner Publications, 2022.

Heos, Bridget. *Treemendous: Diary of a Not Yet Mighty Oak.* New York: Crown Books for Young Readers, 2021.

Karas, G. Brian. *As an Oak Tree Grows.* New York: Nancy Paulsen Books, 2014.

Muller, Gerda. *A Year Around the Great Oak.* Edinburgh: Floris Books, 2019.

Schaefer, Lola M., and Adam Schaefer. *Because of an Acorn.* San Francisco: Chronicle Books, 2016.

ADDITIONAL RESOURCES AND WEBSITES

The Arnold Arboretum of Harvard University: arboretum.harvard.edu/research/

International Oak Society: internationaloaksociety.org/content/oak-conservation-and-research-fund-call-proposals-2024

Kilgore, Georgette. "5 Acorn Tree Types (Identification Guide with Growing Zones)." 8billiontrees, May 17, 2023. 8billiontrees.com/trees/acorn-tree/

The Morton Arboretum, Center for Tree Science: mortonarb.org/science/center-for-tree-science/

Renkl, Margaret. "Why We Should All Be Chasing Acorns." *New York Times,* October 17, 2022. nytimes.com/2022/10/17/opinion/oak-trees-conservation-ecosystems.html.

Rodbarry, Lea. "10 Fascinating Facts About Oak Trees for OAKtober." The Conservation Foundation, October 10, 2023. theconservationfoundation.org/10-fascinating-facts-about-oak-trees-for-oaktober/.

Salhi, Sarah. "The Life of an Oak Tree!" The Green Core, July 14, 2023. thegreencore.org/the-life-of-an-oak-tree/.

Schaefer, James. "Acorn Species Identification Guide." Nut Geeks, December 15, 2022. nutgeeks.com/acorn-identification-guide/.

Shapiro, Leslie. "Why Do Trees Have Differently Shaped Leaves?" *Washington Post,* November 16, 2013. washingtonpost.com/science/interactive/2023/leaf-shape-diversity.

UC Davis Arboretum and Public Garden: arboretum.ucdavis.edu/trees

Will, Melissa J. "About Oak Trees: Natural History, Ecological Benefits, & Mast Years." Empress of Dirt, August 4, 2022. empressofdirt.net/oak-trees/.

We would like to thank
Dr. Douglas W. Tallamy
for reviewing our book and lending his expertise.